THE JOY OF JELL-O® BRAND MOLDS

THE JOY OF
JELL-O® MOLDS

JELL-O Gelatin has a definite place in the hearts of families across America. At picnics, parties, family meals and special occasions, colorful molds are the marks of celebration. Now as we enter a new millennium, JELL-O continues to be a national favorite.

This is your Official JELL-O Mold Recipe Book, filled with tips on making scrumptious, eye-catching creations. This comprehensive guide reveals how to make fruit-filled molds and layered molds with ease, plus how to unmold a masterpiece every time. With just a few ingredients, in just 15 to 20 minutes, you can prepare a sensational salad or dessert mold that is sure to be the marvel of any meal!

This definitive guide has everything you need to inspire you to creative heights. For family gatherings, holiday tables and midweek meals, you can serve delicious JELL-O molds—even when you have little time to prepare.

Join in celebrating our nation's love of JELL-O with these classic favorites and tempting new twists; then experiment with your own concoctions. Whatever shape your JELL-O mold takes, you can count on irresistible results!

© Copyright 1998 Kraft Foods, Inc. and Meredith Corp.
All rights reserved. Canadian BN 12348 2887 RT. Printed in the U.S.A.
Produced by Meredith Integrated Marketing, 1716 Locust St.,
Des Moines, IA 50309-3023.
Printing Number and Year: 5 4 3 2 1   02 01 00 99 98
Library of Congress Catalog Card Number: 98-67490
ISBN: 0-696-20922-5

Kir Royale Mold
(recipe, page 25)

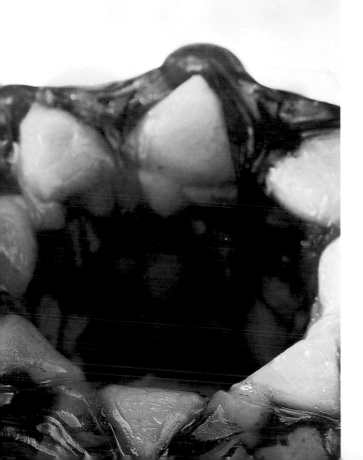

Holiday Fruit and Nut Mold
(recipe, page 24)

Every good cook has her secrets... and these are yours! Even the most elaborate molds are easy when you follow our guidelines for preparing, perfecting and presenting your creations.

SECRETS
FOR SUCCESS

The recipes in *The Joy of JELL-O® Brand Molds* have been developed and tested by the food professionals in the JELL-O Test Kitchens to ensure your success in making them. The following foolproof tips and step-by-step photos will help you get perfect results every time.

Selecting the Mold

- Use metal molds, traditional decorative molds or other forms, or plastic molds. For variety, you can also use square or round cake pans, fluted or plain tube pans, loaf pans, metal mixing bowls (the nested sets give you a variety of sizes) or metal fruit or juice cans (to unmold, dip can in warm water; then puncture bottom of can and unmold). For individual molds, use custard cups, small bowls, soufflé dishes, muffin tins or individual metal or plastic molds.

- To determine the volume of the mold, measure first with water. For clear gelatin, you need a 2-cup mold for a 4-serving size package and a 4-cup mold for an 8-serving size package.

- If the mold holds less than the size called for, pour the extra gelatin into a separate dish. Refrigerate and serve it at another time. Do not use a mold that is too large because the gelatin will be difficult to unmold. Instead, either increase the recipe or use a smaller mold.

Preparing the Mold

- To prepare gelatin for molding, use less water than the amount called for on the package. For a 4-serving size package, decrease cold water to ¾ cup. For an 8-serving size package, decrease cold water to 1½ cups. (This adjustment has already been made in the recipes in this book.) This firmer consistency results in a gelatin mold that is less fragile, so it is easier to unmold.

- For easier unmolding, spray mold with no stick cooking spray before filling mold.

- To prevent spilling, place mold on a tray in the refrigerator before pouring in gelatin.

Tips for Great Molds

- To make a mixture that is clear and uniformly set, be sure the gelatin is completely dissolved in boiling water or other boiling liquid before adding the cold water.

- To double a recipe, double the amounts of gelatin, liquid and other ingredients used, except salt, vinegar and lemon juice. For these ingredients, use 1½ times the amount given in the recipe.

- To arrange fruits or vegetables in the mold, refrigerate gelatin until thickened. (If gelatin

(continued on page 8)

For best results, gelatin needs to be refrigerated to the proper consistency. Use this chart as a guide to determine the desired consistency and the approximate refrigeration time.

WHEN A RECIPE SAYS	IT MEANS GELATIN SHOULD	REFRIGERATION TIME*	USE THIS GELATIN STAGE WHEN
1. Refrigerate until slightly thickened	Be the consistency of unbeaten egg whites	1¼ hours	Adding creamy ingredients or beating the gelatin mixture
2. Refrigerate until thickened	Be thick enough so a spoon drawn through it leaves a definite impression	1½ hours	Adding solid ingredients such as fruits or vegetables
3. Refrigerate until set but not firm	Stick to finger when touched and move to the side when mold is tilted	2 hours	Layering gelatin mixtures
4. Refrigerate until firm	Not stick to finger when touched and not move when mold is tilted	Individual molds: at least 3 hours; 2- to 6-cup mold: at least 4 hours; 8- to 12-cup mold: at least 5 hours or overnight	Unmolding and serving

1. Slightly thickened gelatin should be consistency of unbeaten egg whites.

2. Thickened gelatin should be thick enough so that a spoon drawn through it leaves a definite impression.

3. Set but not firm gelatin should stick to fingers when touched.

4. Firm gelatin should not stick to fingers when touched and should not move when mold is tilted.

*Timings are for metal bowl; allow 10 to 15 minutes more time if using a glass bowl.

is not thick enough, fruits or vegetables may sink or float.) Pour gelatin into mold to about ¼-inch depth. Reserve remaining gelatin at room temperature. Arrange fruits or vegetables in a decorative pattern on the gelatin in the mold. Refrigerate mold until gelatin is set but not firm. Spoon reserved gelatin over pattern in mold. Refrigerate until firm; then unmold.

Creating Layers

- For a clear-and-creamy layered mold, first layer clear gelatin; then top with a layer of gelatin mixed with whipped topping, yogurt, ice cream or cream cheese. Refrigerate each layer only until set but not firm before adding the next layer. If the lower layer is too firm, the layers will not adhere to each other and may slip apart when unmolded. The gelatin should stick to your finger when touched and move gently from side to side when the mold is tilted.

- Except for the first layer, the gelatin mixtures should be cool and slightly thickened before pouring into the mold. A warm mixture could soften the layer beneath it and cause the mixtures to run together.

- To get layers to set at a decorative slant, carefully raise one side of the mold and push a small box of JELL-O Gelatin under the lifted side to support the tilted mold.

- Once all the layers are in the mold, refrigerate several hours or overnight until completely firm. (The gelatin should not feel sticky on top and should not move to the side if mold is tilted.)

- To ensure the mold stays firm when unmolded, chill the serving plate or individual plates on which the mold is to be served.

Serving Molds

- Generally, gelatin molds are best served right from the refrigerator. A gelatin mold containing fruit or vegetables can remain at room temperature for up to 2 hours. Always keep a gelatin mold containing meat, mayonnaise, or dairy products refrigerated until ready to serve. Also, do not let a mold with these ingredients sit at room temperature longer than 30 minutes.

- Always store leftover gelatin in the refrigerator. Cover the gelatin to prevent drying.

After refrigerating the gelatin mold until completely firm, follow these steps for unmolding your mold with ease.

1. Moisten fingertip and gently pull gelatin from top edge of mold. Or, use small metal spatula dipped in warm water to loosen edge.

2. Dip mold in warm, not hot, water, just to rim, for about 15 seconds.

3. Lift mold from water, hold upright and shake to loosen gelatin. Or, gently pull gelatin from edge of mold.

4. Moisten chilled serving plate with water. (This allows gelatin to be moved after unmolding.) Place moistened serving plate upside down on top of mold.

5. Invert mold and plate; holding mold and plate together, shake slightly to loosen.

6. Gently remove mold. If gelatin does not release easily, dip mold in warm water again for a few seconds. Remove mold; center gelatin on serving plate.

Champagne Celebration Mold
(recipe, page 12)

Cranberry Holiday Mold
(recipe, page 13)

FESTIVE
FALL AND WINTER MOLDS

No holiday meal is complete without a shimmering JELL-O mold. Easy to make, yet impressive to behold, these dishes are essential for special gatherings of family and friends.

CHAMPAGNE
CELEBRATION MOLD

"Toast" togetherness with this Sparkling JELL-O mold. For an alcohol-free version, follow the directions below *(photo, pages 10–11)*.

2 cups boiling water

3 packages (4-serving size) JELL-O Brand Sparkling White Grape Flavor Gelatin Dessert

1½ cups cold champagne

1½ cups cold ginger ale

serves **12**
PREP TIME: 10 MIN.
REFRIGERATING TIME: 5¼ HRS.

Stir boiling water into gelatin in large bowl at least 2 minutes until completely dissolved. Refrigerate 15 minutes. Gently stir in cold champagne and ginger ale. Refrigerate about 1 hour or until slightly thickened (consistency of unbeaten egg whites). Gently stir for 30 seconds. Pour into 6-cup mold.

Refrigerate 4 hours or until firm. Unmold. Garnish as desired.

Nonalcoholic Variation: Omit champagne; use 3 cups cold ginger ale.

Note: To prepare with one 8-serving size package gelatin, use 1½ cups boiling water and 1 cup *each* cold champagne and ginger ale. Decrease 1-hour refrigeration time to 30 minutes. Continue as directed above. Makes 8 servings.

Dressing up your holiday table is simple when you prepare this colorful mold. It serves as both salad and centerpiece *(photo, pages 10-11).*

serves **12** PREP TIME: 15 MIN.
REFRIGERATING TIME: 5½ HRS.

Stir boiling water into gelatin in large bowl at least 2 minutes until completely dissolved. Stir in cold ginger ale. Refrigerate about 1½ hours or until thickened (spoon drawn through leaves definite impression).

Stir in grapes and oranges. Pour into 6-cup mold.

Refrigerate 4 hours or until firm. Unmold. Garnish as desired.

2 **cups boiling water**

1 **package (8-serving size)** *or*
   2 packages (4-serving size)
   JELL-O Brand Cranberry
   Flavor Gelatin Dessert

1½ **cups cold ginger ale** *or* **water**

2 **cups green** *and/or* **red grape halves**

1 **can (11 ounces) mandarin orange**
   segments, drained

SPARKLING
FRUIT MOLD

This creation is the perfect addition to a holiday meal. Guests will welcome the light, refreshing combo of fruit and Sparkling JELL-O Gelatin.

1½   **cups boiling water**

1   **package (8-serving size)** *or* **2 packages (4-serving size) JELL-O Brand Sparkling White Grape Flavor Gelatin Dessert**

2   **cups cold ginger ale**

½   **cup** *each* **red and green grape halves**

1   **can (11 ounces) mandarin orange segments, drained**

serves
12

PREP TIME: 15 MIN.
REFRIGERATING TIME: 4¾ HRS.

Stir boiling water into gelatin in large bowl at least 2 minutes until completely dissolved. Refrigerate 15 minutes. Gently stir in cold ginger ale. Refrigerate about 30 minutes or until slightly thickened (consistency of unbeaten egg whites). Gently stir for 15 seconds. Stir in grapes and oranges. Pour into 6-cup mold.

Refrigerate 4 hours or until firm. Unmold. Garnish as desired.

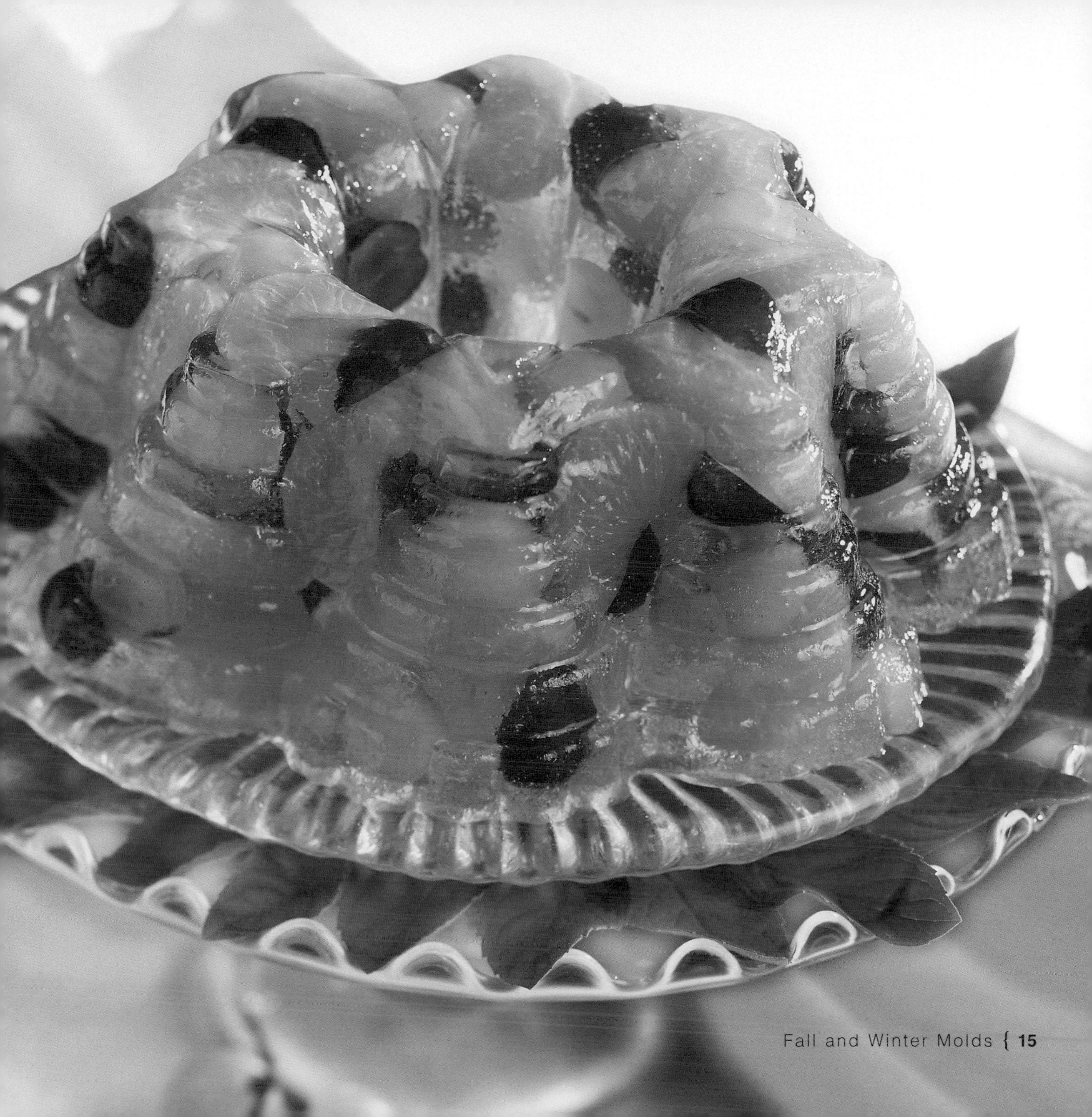

SPICED
CRANBERRY-ORANGE MOLD

Cranberries are dressed in holiday splendor to steal the show at your turkey dinner. Garnish the mold with fresh cranberries and oranges.

1½ **cups boiling water**

1 **package (8-serving size) *or*
2 packages (4-serving size) JELL-O
Brand Cranberry Flavor Gelatin
Dessert *or* any red fruit flavor**

½ **teaspoon ground cinnamon**

1 **can (16 ounces) whole berry
cranberry sauce**

1 **cup cold water**

1 **orange, sectioned, diced**

½ **cup chopped walnuts, toasted**

serves **12**

PREP TIME: 15 MIN.
REFRIGERATING TIME: 5½ HRS.

Stir boiling water into gelatin and cinnamon in large bowl at least 2 minutes until completely dissolved. Stir in cranberry sauce until melted. Stir in cold water. Refrigerate about 1½ hours or until thickened (spoon drawn through leaves definite impression).

Stir in orange and walnuts. Pour into 6-cup mold.

Refrigerate 4 hours or until firm. Unmold. Garnish as desired.

This pink-and-white mold adds elegance to any menu, especially a holiday open house, Valentine's dinner or wedding shower buffet.

serves **10** PREP TIME: 15 MIN.
REFRIGERATING TIME: 5½ HRS.

Bring 2 cups water and mints to boil in small saucepan on medium heat, stirring constantly until mints are dissolved. Stir mint mixture into gelatin in large bowl at least 2 minutes until completely dissolved. Stir in cold water. Pour 3 cups of the gelatin into 6-cup mold. Refrigerate about 1½ hours or until set but not firm (should stick to finger when touched).

Meanwhile, reserve remaining gelatin at room temperature for 45 minutes. Refrigerate about 45 minutes or until slightly thickened (consistency of unbeaten egg whites). Gently stir in whipped topping with wire whisk until smooth. Spoon over gelatin layer in mold.

Refrigerate 4 hours or until firm. Unmold. Garnish as desired.

2   **cups water**

14   **red starlight mints**

1   **package (8-serving size)** *or*
**2 packages (4-serving size)
JELL-O Brand Raspberry Flavor
Gelatin Dessert**

1½   **cups cold water**

2   **cups thawed COOL WHIP
Whipped Topping**

CRANBERRY
CREAM CHEESE MOLD

This picture-perfect layered mold is a tasty way
to celebrate a fruitful harvest.

1½ cups boiling water

1 package (8-serving size) *or*
2 packages (4-serving size) JELL-O
Brand Cranberry Flavor Gelatin
Dessert *or* any red fruit flavor

1½ cups cold water

½ teaspoon ground cinnamon

1 medium apple, chopped

1 cup whole berry cranberry sauce

1 package (8 ounces) PHILADELPHIA
Cream Cheese, softened

serves **12** PREP TIME: 20 MIN.
REFRIGERATING TIME: 5¾ HRS.

Stir boiling water into gelatin in large bowl at
least 2 minutes until completely dissolved.
Stir in cold water and cinnamon. Reserve
1 cup gelatin at room temperature. Refrigerate
remaining gelatin about 1¼ hours or until
thickened (spoon drawn through leaves
definite impression).

Stir apple and cranberry sauce into thickened
gelatin. Spoon into 6-cup mold. Refrigerate
about 30 minutes or until set but not firm
(should stick to finger when touched).

Beat reserved 1 cup gelatin gradually into
cream cheese in medium bowl with wire
whisk until smooth. Pour over gelatin layer
in mold.

Refrigerate 4 hours or until firm. Unmold.
Garnish as desired.

CHERRY
ROYALE

This fruit-filled mold deserves a place on any holiday buffet. Its creamy red color and sweet cherries are perfect party pleasers.

1 can (16 ounces) pitted dark sweet cherries in syrup, undrained

Cold water

2 cups boiling water

1 package (8-serving size) *or* 2 packages (4-serving size) JELL-O Brand Cherry Flavor Gelatin Dessert

1 cup thawed COOL WHIP Whipped Topping

serves **12**

PREP TIME: 20 MIN.
REFRIGERATING TIME: 5½ HRS.

Drain cherries, reserving syrup. Add cold water to syrup to measure 1½ cups. Cut cherries in half. Stir boiling water into gelatin in large bowl at least 2 minutes until completely dissolved. Stir in measured syrup and water. Reserve 2 cups gelatin at room temperature. Refrigerate remaining gelatin about 1 hour or until thickened (spoon drawn through leaves definite impression).

Stir in cherries. Pour into 6-cup mold. Refrigerate about 30 minutes or until set but not firm (should stick to finger when touched). Refrigerate reserved 2 cups gelatin 30 minutes.

Gently stir whipped topping into reserved 2 cups gelatin with wire whisk until smooth. Pour over gelatin layer in mold.

Refrigerate 4 hours or until firm. Unmold. Garnish as desired.

Creamy JELL-O pudding and rum extract are the secrets behind this novel New Year's treat—perfect for midnight celebrations.

serves **10**

PREP TIME: 25 MIN.
REFRIGERATING TIME: 4 1/4 HRS.

Stir boiling water into gelatin in large bowl at least 2 minutes until completely dissolved. Stir in cold water. Cool 30 minutes to room temperature.

Pour milk into medium bowl. Add pudding mix. Beat with wire whisk 30 seconds. Immediately stir into cooled gelatin until smooth. Stir in rum extract and nutmeg. Refrigerate about 15 minutes or until slightly thickened (consistency of unbeaten egg whites). Gently stir in whipped topping with wire whisk until smooth. Pour into 5-cup mold.

Refrigerate 4 hours or until firm. Unmold. Garnish as desired.

1 1/2 **cups boiling water**

1 **package (8-serving size) *or*
2 packages (4-serving size) JELL-O
Brand Lemon Flavor Gelatin Dessert**

1/2 **cup cold water**

1 1/2 **cups cold milk**

1 **package (4-serving size) JELL-O
Vanilla Flavor Instant Pudding &
Pie Filling**

2 **teaspoons rum extract**

1/2 **teaspoon ground nutmeg**

2 **cups thawed COOL WHIP
Whipped Topping**

Looking just like a package, this beautifully garnished mold makes an eye-catching centerpiece for any birthday party or shower.

serves 12 PREP TIME: 15 MIN.
REFRIGERATING TIME: 4 HRS.

Stir boiling water into gelatin in large bowl at least 2 minutes until completely dissolved. Stir in ice cream until melted and smooth. Gently stir in 8 ounces whipped topping with wire whisk until smooth. Pour into 9x5-inch loaf pan.

Refrigerate 4 hours or until firm. Unmold. Pipe on additional whipped topping or decorate with chewy fruit snack roll to resemble ribbon and bow. Garnish as desired.

2   **cups boiling water**

1   **package (8-serving size)** *or*
    **2 packages (4-serving size) JELL-O
    Brand Raspberry Flavor Gelatin
    Dessert** *or* **any red fruit flavor**

1   **pint (2 cups) vanilla ice cream,
    softened**

1   **tub (8 ounces) COOL WHIP Whipped
    Topping, thawed**

    **Thawed COOL WHIP Whipped
    Topping** *or* **chewy fruit snack roll**

HOLIDAY
FRUIT
AND NUT MOLD

For a decorative touch, arrange cutouts of dried fruit in the mold before spooning in the gelatin mixture *(photo, pages 4–5)*.

serves 10

PREP TIME: 20 MIN.
REFRIGERATING TIME: 5½ HRS.

2 cups boiling water

1 package (8-serving size) *or*
2 packages (4-serving size) JELL-O
Brand Gelatin Dessert, any flavor

1¼ cups cold ginger ale *or* carbonated
lemon-lime beverage

⅛ teaspoon *each* ground cinnamon,
cloves and nutmeg

½ cup chopped mixed dried fruit

⅓ cup currants *or* golden raisins

⅓ cup chopped candied *or*
maraschino cherries

⅓ cup chopped pecans *or*
walnuts, toasted

Stir boiling water into gelatin in large bowl at least 2 minutes until completely dissolved. Stir in cold ginger ale and spices. Refrigerate about 1½ hours or until thickened (spoon drawn through leaves definite impression).

Stir in fruits and pecans. Spoon into 5-cup mold.

Refrigerate 4 hours or until firm. Unmold. Garnish as desired.

This Sparkling mold rises to any occasion with definitive fruit flavors and a splash of crème de cassis liqueur *(photo, pages 4–5)*.

serves
12

PREP TIME: 15 MIN.
REFRIGERATING TIME: 4¾ HRS.

Stir boiling water into gelatin in large bowl at least 2 minutes until completely dissolved. Refrigerate 15 minutes. Gently stir in cold club soda and liqueur. Refrigerate about 30 minutes or until slightly thickened (consistency of unbeaten egg whites). Gently stir for 15 seconds. Stir in raspberries. Pour into 6-cup mold.

Refrigerate 4 hours or until firm. Unmold. Garnish as desired.

2 **cups boiling water**

1 **package (8-serving size) *or*
2 packages (4-serving size) JELL-O Brand Sparkling White Grape *or* Sparkling Wild Berry Flavor Gelatin Dessert**

1½ **cups cold club soda, seltzer *or* champagne**

2 **tablespoons crème de cassis liqueur (optional)**

2 **cups raspberries**

American Red-White-and-Blue Mold
(recipe, page 36) and Lemon Mousse
with Raspberry Sauce (recipe, page 29)

REFRESHING
MOLDS FOR SPRING AND SUMMER

Whether it's Mother's Day, a graduation, the Fourth of July or just a family meal, the occasion will shine brighter with one of these dazzling molds as the star.

FRESH FRUIT
PARFAIT
MOLD

To make individual parfaits, divide the layers evenly among parfait glasses instead of using a large mold *(photo on cover)*.

serves **12**

PREP TIME: 15 MIN.
REFRIGERATING TIME: 5½ HRS.

1½ **cups boiling water**

1 **package (8-serving size) *or* 2 packages (4-serving size) JELL-O Brand Strawberry Flavor Gelatin Dessert**

1½ **cups cold water**

¾ **cup *each* blueberries *and* chopped strawberries**

1½ **cups thawed COOL WHIP Whipped Topping**

Stir boiling water into gelatin in large bowl at least 2 minutes until completely dissolved. Stir in cold water. Refrigerate about 1¼ hours or until slightly thickened (consistency of unbeaten egg whites). Reserve 1½ cups of the gelatin at room temperature.

Stir fruit into remaining gelatin. Spoon into 6-cup mold. Refrigerate 15 minutes or until set but not firm (should stick to finger when touched).

Gently stir whipped topping into reserved 1½ cups gelatin with wire whisk until smooth. Spoon over gelatin layer in mold.

Refrigerate 4 hours or until firm. Unmold. Garnish as desired.

LEMON
MOUSSE
WITH RASPBERRY SAUCE

Serve this luscious citrus mold as a brunch finale, a light dessert after a filling meal or a special treat anytime *(photo, pages 26–27).*

serves **12** PREP TIME: 15 MIN.
REFRIGERATING TIME: 4¼ HRS.

Stir boiling water into gelatin and lemon peel in large bowl at least 2 minutes until gelatin is completely dissolved. Stir in cold water and orange juice. Refrigerate about 1¼ hours or until slightly thickened (consistency of unbeaten egg whites).

Gently stir in whipped topping with wire whisk until smooth. Pour into 12 individual (6-ounce) molds or custard cups, filling each about ¾ full. (Or, pour into 6-cup mold.)

Refrigerate 3 hours or until firm. Unmold. Serve with raspberry puree. Garnish as desired.

1½ **cups boiling water**

1 **package (8-serving size) *or* 2 packages (4-serving size) JELL-O Brand Lemon Flavor Gelatin Dessert**

2 **teaspoons grated lemon peel**

1 **cup cold water**

¾ **cup cold orange juice**

1 **tub (8 ounces) COOL WHIP Whipped Topping, thawed**

1 **package (10 ounces) frozen raspberries *or* strawberries in syrup, thawed, pureed in blender**

MIMOSA
SPARKLING MOLD

Turn this marvelous Sparkling mold out onto a
glass platter and garnish with a strawberry fan
for an easy spring or summer salute.

serves **12**

PREP TIME: 15 MIN.
REFRIGERATING TIME: 4 3/4 HRS.

Stir boiling water into gelatin in large bowl at
least 2 minutes until completely dissolved.
Refrigerate 15 minutes. Gently stir in cold
club soda. Refrigerate about 30 minutes
or until slightly thickened (consistency of
unbeaten egg whites). Gently stir for
15 seconds. Stir in oranges and strawberries.
Pour into 6-cup mold.

Refrigerate 4 hours or until firm. Unmold.
Garnish as desired.

1 1/2 cups boiling water

1 package (8-serving size) *or*
2 packages (4-serving size) JELL-O
Brand Sparkling White Grape Flavor
Gelatin Dessert

2 cups cold club soda *or* seltzer

1 can (11 ounces) mandarin orange
segments, drained

1 cup sliced strawberries

SUMMER
FRUIT BASKET

Showcase the summer's best fresh fruit with your favorite JELL-O Gelatin fruit flavor. This pleaser goes fast at picnics and barbecues!

2 cups boiling water

1 package (8-serving size) *or* 2 packages (4-serving size) JELL-O Brand Strawberry Flavor Gelatin Dessert *or* any red fruit flavor

1½ cups cold ginger ale *or* water

1 cup sliced strawberries

1 cup green grape halves

1 cup cantaloupe cubes

serves **12**

PREP TIME: 20 MIN.
REFRIGERATING TIME: 5½ HRS.

Stir boiling water into gelatin in large bowl at least 2 minutes until completely dissolved. Stir in cold ginger ale. Refrigerate about 1½ hours or until thickened (spoon drawn through leaves definite impression).

Stir in fruit. Pour into 6-cup mold.

Refrigerate 4 hours or until firm. Unmold. Garnish as desired.

The maraschino cherries in this wonderfully refreshing mold add a festive touch for showers, graduations and sunny celebrations.

serves 12 PREP TIME: 20 MIN.
REFRIGERATING TIME: 5¼ HRS.

Stir boiling water into gelatin in large bowl at least 2 minutes until completely dissolved. Stir in pineapple with juice. Refrigerate about 1¼ hours or until slightly thickened (consistency of unbeaten egg whites).

Stir cottage cheese into cream cheese in separate bowl until well blended. Gently stir in whipped topping until smooth. Beat into slightly thickened gelatin with wire whisk until well blended. Stir in walnuts and cherries. Pour into 6-cup mold.

Refrigerate 4 hours or until firm. Unmold. Serve on greens, if desired.

Note: Soften cream cheese in microwave on HIGH 15 to 20 seconds.

1½ **cups boiling water**

1 **package (8-serving size)** *or* **2 packages (4-serving size) JELL-O Brand Lime Flavor Gelatin Dessert**

1 **can (8 ounces) crushed pineapple in juice, undrained**

1 **cup LIGHT N' LIVELY Lowfat Cottage Cheese with Calcium**

1 **package (8 ounces) PHILADELPHIA Cream Cheese, softened**

1 **cup thawed COOL WHIP Whipped Topping**

½ **cup chopped walnuts**

¼ **cup chopped maraschino cherries**

Salad greens (optional)

TRIPLE
BERRY MOLD

Bring home berries from a farmers' market or berry patch for this Sparkling delight. Three kinds of berries bring surprise in every bite.

1½   cups boiling water

1   package (8-serving size) *or*
    2 packages (4-serving size) JELL-O
    Brand Sparkling Wild Berry Flavor
    Gelatin Dessert

2   cups cold club soda *or* seltzer

2   cups assorted berries (blueberries,
    raspberries and sliced strawberries)

serves
12   PREP TIME: 15 MIN.
        REFRIGERATING TIME: 4³/₄ HRS.

Stir boiling water into gelatin in large bowl at least 2 minutes until completely dissolved. Refrigerate 15 minutes. Gently stir in cold club soda. Refrigerate about 30 minutes or until slightly thickened (consistency of unbeaten egg whites). Gently stir for 15 seconds. Stir in berries. Pour into 6-cup mold.

Refrigerate 4 hours or until firm. Unmold. Garnish as desired.

AMERICAN

RED-WHITE-AND-BLUE MOLD

This patriotic medley of strawberries, JELL-O Gelatin and ice cream is great for Fourth of July parties *(photo, pages 26–27)*.

3   **cups boiling water**

1   **package (4-serving size) JELL-O Brand Strawberry Flavor Gelatin Dessert *or* any red fruit flavor**

1   **package (4-serving size) JELL-O Brand Berry Blue Flavor Gelatin Dessert**

1   **cup cold water**

1½   **cups sliced strawberries**

1   **package (4-serving size) JELL-O Brand Sparkling White Grape *or* Lemon Flavor Gelatin Dessert**

1   **cup vanilla ice cream, softened**

1½   **cups blueberries**

serves **12** PREP TIME: 45 MIN.
REFRIGERATING TIME: 4½ HRS.

Stir 1 cup of the boiling water into each of the strawberry and berry blue gelatins in separate medium bowls at least 2 minutes until completely dissolved. Stir in ½ cup of the cold water into each bowl. Place bowl of strawberry gelatin in larger bowl of ice and water. Stir until thickened, about 8 minutes. Stir in strawberries. Pour into 8-cup mold. Refrigerate 8 minutes or until set but not firm (should stick to finger when touched).

Meanwhile, stir remaining 1 cup boiling water into sparkling white grape or lemon gelatin in medium bowl at least 2 minutes until completely dissolved. Stir in ice cream until smooth. Spoon over strawberry gelatin layer in mold. Refrigerate 10 minutes.

Meanwhile, place bowl of berry blue gelatin in larger bowl of ice and water. Stir until thickened, about 7 minutes. Stir in blueberries. Spoon over gelatin in mold. Refrigerate 4 hours or overnight until firm. Unmold.

For warm weather get-togethers, serve this salad as an easy complement to kabobs or teriyaki chicken.

serves **10**

PREP TIME: 20 MIN.
REFRIGERATING TIME: 6 HRS.

Drain pineapple, reserving juice. Add cold water to juice to make 1½ cups.

Stir boiling water into gelatin in large bowl at least 2 minutes until completely dissolved. Stir in measured pineapple juice and water. Reserve 1 cup gelatin at room temperature.

Stir ½ of the crushed pineapple into remaining gelatin. Pour into 6-cup mold. Refrigerate about 2 hours or until set but not firm (should stick to finger when touched).

Stir reserved 1 cup gelatin gradually into cream cheese in medium bowl with wire whisk until smooth. Stir in remaining crushed pineapple. Pour over gelatin layer in mold.

Refrigerate 4 hours or until firm. Unmold. Garnish as desired.

1   can (20 ounces) crushed pineapple in juice, undrained

Cold water

1½ cups boiling water

1   package (8-serving size) *or* 2 packages (4-serving size) JELL-O Brand Orange Flavor Gelatin Dessert

1   package (8 ounces) PHILADELPHIA Cream Cheese, softened

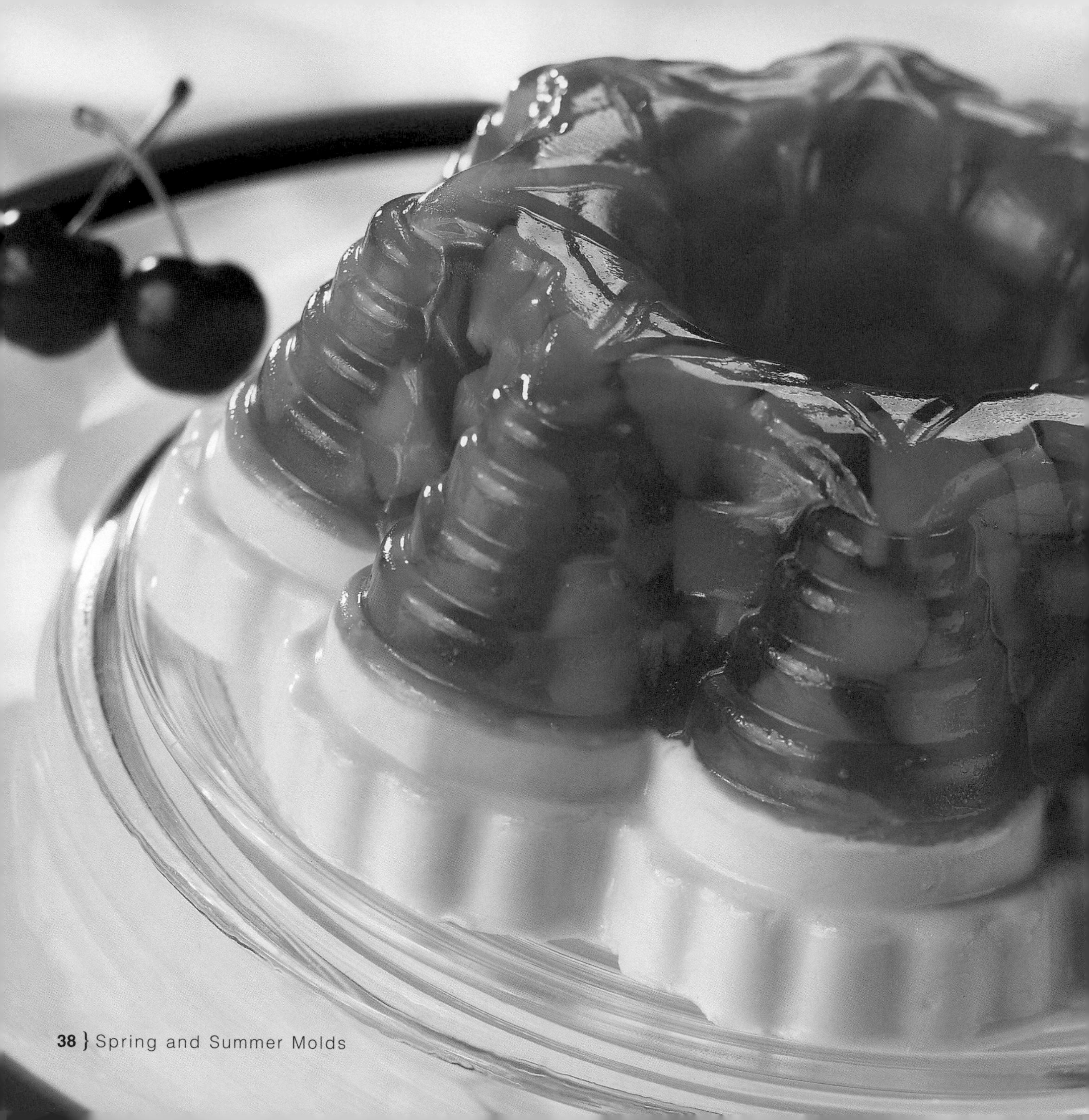

JELL-O teams up with PHILADELPHIA Cream Cheese for a mold that's blooming with bursts of orange and peach.

serves **12** PREP TIME: 20 MIN.
REFRIGERATING TIME: 5 1/4 HRS.

Stir boiling water into gelatin in large bowl at least 2 minutes until completely dissolved. Stir in cold water. Reserve 1 1/2 cups gelatin at room temperature.

Stir peaches into remaining gelatin. Pour into 6-cup mold. Refrigerate about 1 1/4 hours or until set but not firm (should stick to finger when touched).

Beat reserved 1 1/2 cups gelatin gradually into cream cheese in medium bowl with wire whisk until smooth. Stir in oranges. Pour over gelatin layer in mold.

Refrigerate 4 hours or until firm. Unmold. Garnish as desired.

1 1/2 **cups boiling water**

1 **package (8-serving size)** *or* **2 packages (4-serving size) JELL-O Brand Orange Flavor Gelatin Dessert**

1 1/2 **cups cold water**

1 **can (16 ounces) peach slices in syrup, drained, diced**

1 **package (8 ounces) PHILADELPHIA Cream Cheese, softened**

1 **can (11 ounces) mandarin orange segments, drained**

STRAWBERRY
SOUFFLÉ

This refreshing, creamy mold is sure to be the easiest soufflé you'll make—and probably the most popular.

1½   cups boiling water

1   package (8-serving size) *or*
2 packages (4-serving size) JELL-O Brand Strawberry Flavor Gelatin Dessert

1   package (10 ounces) strawberries in syrup, thawed, pureed and strained

1   cup cold water

2   cups thawed COOL WHIP Whipped Topping

serves
12

PREP TIME: 15 MIN.
REFRIGERATING TIME: 5 HRS.

Stir boiling water into gelatin in large bowl at least 2 minutes until completely dissolved. Stir in strawberry puree and cold water. Refrigerate about 1 hour or until slightly thickened (consistency of unbeaten egg whites).

Gently stir in whipped topping with wire whisk until smooth. Pour into 6-cup mold.

Refrigerate 4 hours or until firm. Unmold. Garnish as desired.

Serve this salad surrounded with an assortment of cold cuts, cheeses and vegetables for a luscious, light lunch or supper.

serves **8**

PREP TIME: 15 MIN.
REFRIGERATING TIME: 5½ HRS.

Stir boiling water into gelatin in large bowl at least 2 minutes until completely dissolved. Stir in tomato juice, lemon juice, Worcestershire sauce and dill weed. Refrigerate about 1½ hours or until thickened (spoon drawn through leaves definite impression).

Stir in celery. Pour into a 5-cup mold.

Refrigerate 4 hours or until firm. Unmold. Serve on salad greens, if desired.

2 cups boiling water

1 package (8-serving size) *or* 2 packages (4-serving size) JELL-O Brand Lemon Flavor Gelatin Dessert

1½ cups tomato juice

2 teaspoons lemon juice

2 teaspoons Worcestershire sauce

1 teaspoon dried dill weed

1 cup diced celery

Double Orange and Cream Mold *(recipe, page 44)* and Florida Sunshine Citrus Salad *(recipe, page 45)*

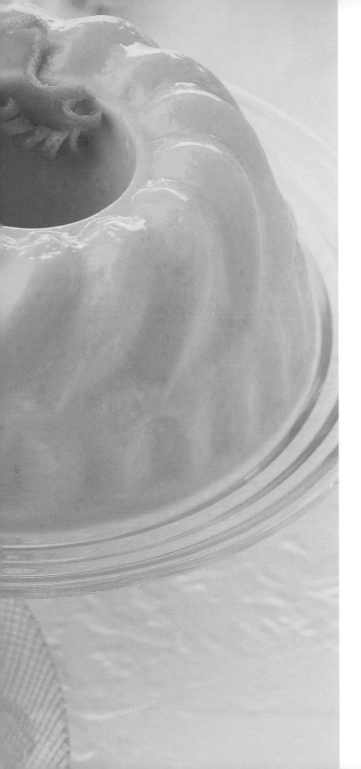

Keep the pantry stocked with handy JELL-O Gelatin and you'll be ready to stir up a salad anytime.

DOUBLE
ORANGE
AND CREAM MOLD

With ice cream in the mix, this creamy concoction is reminiscent of old-fashioned ice cream treats (photo, pages 42–43).

2 cups boiling water

1 package (8-serving size) *or*
2 packages (4-serving size) JELL-O Brand Orange Flavor Gelatin Dessert

1 cup cold orange juice

1 pint (2 cups) vanilla ice cream, softened

serves
10

PREP TIME: 10 MIN.
REFRIGERATING TIME: 4 HRS.

Stir boiling water into gelatin in large bowl at least 2 minutes until completely dissolved. Stir in cold orange juice. Stir in ice cream until melted and smooth. Pour into 5-cup mold.

Refrigerate 4 hours or until firm. Unmold. Garnish as desired.

Carbonated lemon-lime beverage, citrus peel and citrus sections add just the right zest to this JELL-O salad *(photo, pages 42–43)*.

serves **10** PREP TIME: 15 MIN.
REFRIGERATING TIME: 5½ HRS.

Stir boiling water into gelatin in large bowl at least 2 minutes until completely dissolved. Stir in cold lemon-lime beverage and lemon peel. Refrigerate about 1½ hours or until thickened (spoon drawn through leaves definite impression).

Stir in fruit. Pour into 6-cup mold.

Refrigerate 4 hours or until firm. Unmold. Garnish as desired.

1½ **cups boiling water**

1 **package (8-serving size)** *or*
2 packages (4-serving size) JELL-O Brand Lemon Flavor Gelatin Dessert

2 **cups cold carbonated lemon-lime beverage**

2 **teaspoons grated lemon peel**

2 **cups diced orange** *and/or* **grapefruit sections**

STRAWBERRY
BANANA SALAD

Two classic flavors come together to make this favorite family fare. For a simple garnish, use sliced star fruit, bananas and berries.

serves
10

PREP TIME: 15 MIN.
REFRIGERATING TIME: 5½ HRS.

Stir boiling water into gelatin in large bowl at least 2 minutes until completely dissolved. Stir in cold water. Refrigerate about 1½ hours or until thickened (spoon drawn through leaves definite impression).

Stir in strawberries and banana. Pour into 5-cup mold.

Refrigerate 4 hours or until firm. Unmold. Garnish as desired.

1½ **cups boiling water**

1 **package (8-serving size)** *or*
**2 packages (4-serving size) JELL-O
Brand Strawberry** *or* **Strawberry
Banana Flavor Gelatin Dessert**

2 **cups cold water**

1 **cup chopped strawberries**

1 **banana, sliced**

APPLE
ORCHARD MOLD

Apples lend a nice crunch to this salad, which is delicious with roast pork or turkey.

1½   **cups boiling water**

1   **package (8-serving size)** *or*
**2 packages (4-serving size) JELL-O
Brand Lemon Flavor Gelatin Dessert**

2   **cups cold apple juice**

1   *each* **small red and green apple,
diced**

Stir boiling water into gelatin in large bowl at least 2 minutes until completely dissolved. Stir in cold apple juice. Refrigerate about 1½ hours or until thickened (spoon drawn through leaves definite impression).

Stir in apples. Pour into 6-cup mold.

Refrigerate 4 hours or until firm. Unmold. Garnish as desired.

Can't decide which flavor you favor? Experiment with different fruit tastes—and colors—by changing the JELL-O Gelatin flavor.

serves
12
PREP TIME: 10 MIN.
REFRIGERATING TIME: 5½ HRS.

Stir boiling water into gelatin in large bowl at least 2 minutes until completely dissolved. Stir in cold lemon-lime beverage. Refrigerate 1½ hours or until thickened (spoon drawn through leaves definite impression).

Stir in fruit cocktail. Pour into 6-cup mold.

Refrigerate 4 hours or until firm. Unmold. Garnish as desired.

1½ **cups boiling water**

1 **package (8-serving size)** *or*
   2 packages (4-serving size) JELL-O
   Brand Gelatin Dessert, any fruit flavor

2 **cups cold carbonated lemon-lime**
   beverage *or* **water**

1 **can (30 ounces) fruit cocktail,**
   drained

For a mini-celebration—good grades or a finished project—present this Sparkling mold for dinner.

serves 12 PREP TIME: 15 MIN.
REFRIGERATING TIME: 4½ HRS.

1½ **cups boiling water**

1 **package (8-serving size)** *or*
2 packages (4-serving size) JELL-O Brand Sparkling Wild Berry Flavor Gelatin Dessert

1 **cup frozen raspberries**

2 **cups cold carbonated lemon-lime beverage**

1 **can (16 ounces) pear halves in syrup, drained, diced**

Stir boiling water into gelatin in large bowl at least 2 minutes until completely dissolved. Add frozen raspberries; stir until thawed. Gently stir in cold lemon-lime beverage. Refrigerate about 30 minutes or until slightly thickened (consistency of unbeaten egg whites). Gently stir for 15 seconds. Stir in pears. Pour into 6-cup mold.

Refrigerate 4 hours or until firm. Unmold. Garnish as desired.

CHERRY
PINEAPPLE MOLD

Maraschino cherries make this salad a winner with the kids. Keep it on hand for something you know they'll always enjoy.

1   can (20 ounces) pineapple chunks in juice, undrained

Cold water

2   cups boiling water

1   package (8-serving size) *or* 2 packages (4-serving size) JELL-O Brand Cherry Flavor Gelatin Dessert

½   cup diced maraschino cherries

serves
12

PREP TIME: 15 MIN.
REFRIGERATING TIME: 5½ HRS.

Drain pineapple, reserving juice. Add cold water to juice to measure 1½ cups. Stir boiling water into gelatin in large bowl at least 2 minutes until completely dissolved. Stir in measured pineapple juice and water. Refrigerate about 1½ hours or until thickened (spoon drawn through leaves definite impression).

Stir in pineapple and cherries. Pour into 6-cup mold.

Refrigerate 4 hours or until firm. Unmold. Garnish as desired.

Canned peaches and whipped topping make this mold easy to prepare anytime, yet special enough for any celebration.

serves 10

PREP TIME: 15 MIN.
REFRIGERATING TIME: 5 ½ HRS.

Drain peaches, reserving syrup. Add cold water to syrup to measure 1½ cups. Dice peaches. Stir boiling water into gelatin in large bowl at least 2 minutes until completely dissolved. Stir in measured syrup and water. Refrigerate about 1¼ hours or until slightly thickened (consistency of unbeaten egg whites).

Gently stir in whipped topping with wire whisk until smooth. Refrigerate about 15 minutes or until thickened (spoon drawn through leaves definite impression). Stir in peaches. Pour into 5-cup mold.

Refrigerate 4 hours or until firm. Unmold. Garnish as desired.

1   **can (16 ounces) peach slices in syrup, undrained**

    Cold water

1½   **cups boiling water**

1   **package (8-serving size) or 2 packages (4-serving size) JELL-O Brand Peach or Orange Flavor Gelatin Dessert**

2   **cups thawed COOL WHIP Whipped Topping**

Peach Melba Salad *(recipe, page 56)* and Melon Duo Salad *(recipe, page 57)*

LUSCIOUS AND
LIGHT
SALADS

Sugar Free Low Calorie JELL-O Gelatin, luscious fruit and flavors from around the world make fabulous salads. If you're watching what you eat, turn to these refreshing salads.

As the dessert classic for which this salad is named shows, peaches and raspberries make a perfect pair *(photo, pages 54–55)*.

serves 8

PREP TIME: 20 MIN.
REFRIGERATING TIME: 5½ HRS.

1 can (8 ounces) peach slices in juice, undrained

Cold water

1½ cups boiling water

2 packages (4-serving size) JELL-O Brand Raspberry Flavor Sugar Free Low Calorie Gelatin Dessert

1 container (8 ounces) vanilla lowfat yogurt

1 cup raspberries, divided

NUTRITION INFORMATION PER SERVING: 60 calories, 0 g fat, less than 5 mg cholesterol, 75 mg sodium, 10 g carbohydrate, 1 g dietary fiber, 11 g sugars, 3 g protein

Drain peaches, reserving juice. Add cold water to reserved juice to make 1 cup. Stir ¾ cup of the boiling water into 1 package of gelatin in medium bowl at least 2 minutes until completely dissolved. Stir in measured juice and water. Refrigerate about 45 minutes or until slightly thickened (consistency of unbeaten egg whites).

Reserve several peach slices for garnish; chop remaining peaches. Stir chopped peaches into slightly thickened gelatin. Spoon into two 2½-cup molds or one 5-cup mold. Refrigerate about 45 minutes or until set but not firm (should stick to finger when touched).

Meanwhile, stir remaining ¾ cup boiling water into remaining package of gelatin in medium bowl at least 2 minutes until completely dissolved. Refrigerate about 30 minutes or until slightly thickened (consistency of unbeaten egg whites). Stir in yogurt and ½ cup of the raspberries. Spoon over gelatin layer in mold.

Refrigerate 4 hours or until firm. Unmold. Garnish with reserved peach slices and remaining ½ cup raspberries.

Melon lovers marvel at this fruity creation made with flavorful, colorful honeydew and cantaloupe balls *(photo, pages 54–55)*.

serves **10** PREP TIME: 15 MIN.
REFRIGERATING TIME: 5½ HRS.

Stir boiling apple juice into gelatin in large bowl at least 2 minutes until completely dissolved. Stir in cold club soda and lemon juice. Refrigerate about 1½ hours or until thickened (spoon drawn through leaves definite impression).

Stir in melon balls. Spoon into 6-cup mold.

Refrigerate 4 hours or until firm. Unmold. Garnish as desired.

2½ **cups boiling apple juice**

1 **package (8-serving size) *or*
2 packages (4-serving size) JELL-O
Brand Lemon Flavor Sugar Free
Low Calorie Gelatin Dessert**

1½ **cups cold club soda *or* seltzer**

1 **teaspoon lemon juice**

1 **cup cantaloupe balls**

1 **cup honeydew melon balls**

NUTRITION INFORMATION PER SERVING: 50 calories,
0 g fat, 0 mg cholesterol, 60 mg sodium,
10 g carbohydrate, 0 g dietary fiber, 10 g sugars,
1 g protein, 20% daily value vitamin C

Cranberry juice cocktail adds zing to this "berry" delicious treat. For an elegant flavor boost, add crème de cassis liqueur.

2 cups boiling diet cranberry juice cocktail

1 package (8-serving size) *or* 2 packages (4-serving size) JELL-O Brand Sugar Free Low Calorie Gelatin Dessert, any red fruit flavor

1½ cups cold club soda *or* seltzer

¼ cup crème de cassis liqueur (optional)

1 teaspoon lemon juice

2 cups assorted berries (blueberries, raspberries and sliced strawberries)

NUTRITION INFORMATION PER SERVING (using liqueur): 40 calories, 0 g fat, 0 mg cholesterol, 90 mg sodium, 7 g carbohydrate, 1 g dietary fiber, 6 g sugars, 2 g protein, 45% daily value vitamin C

serves **8**
PREP TIME: 15 MIN.
REFRIGERATING TIME: 5½ HRS.

Stir boiling cranberry juice into gelatin in large bowl at least 2 minutes until completely dissolved. Stir in cold club soda, liqueur and lemon juice. Refrigerate about 1½ hours or until thickened (spoon drawn through leaves definite impression).

Stir in berries. Spoon into two 3-cup molds or one 5-cup mold.

Refrigerate 4 hours or until firm. Unmold. Garnish as desired.

CIDER
CRANBERRY MOLD

Perfect for any special occasion, this mold is as festive as it is scrumptious. If you like, top it off with a dollop of lite whipped topping.

2 **cups boiling apple juice *or* apple cider**

1 **package (8-serving size) *or* 2 packages (4-serving size) JELL-O Brand Cranberry Flavor Sugar Free Low Calorie Gelatin Dessert *or* any red fruit flavor**

1½ **cups diet cranberry juice cocktail**

NUTRITION INFORMATION PER SERVING (using apple juice): 45 calories, 0 g fat, 0 mg cholesterol, 80 mg sodium, 10 g carbohydrate, 0 g dietary fiber, 9 g sugars, 1 g protein

serves
8

PREP TIME: 10 MIN.
REFRIGERATING TIME: 4 HRS.

Stir boiling cider into gelatin in large bowl at least 2 minutes until completely dissolved. Stir in cranberry juice. Pour into 4-cup mold.

Refrigerate 4 hours or until firm. Unmold. Garnish as desired.

When the sun sets, appetites rise for this cranberry and orange sensation. It goes well with roast chicken or ham.

serves **10**

PREP TIME: 20 MIN.
REFRIGERATING TIME: 5 HRS.

Stir 1 cup of the boiling water into cranberry gelatin in medium bowl at least 2 minutes until completely dissolved. Stir in cold water. Refrigerate about 45 minutes or until slightly thickened (consistency of unbeaten egg whites). Stir in peaches. Spoon into 5-cup mold. Refrigerate about 15 minutes or until set but not firm (should stick to finger when touched).

Meanwhile, stir remaining 1 cup boiling water into orange gelatin in medium bowl at least 2 minutes until completely dissolved. Stir in pineapple with juice. Pour over gelatin layer in mold.

Refrigerate 4 hours or until firm. Unmold. Garnish as desired.

2 cups boiling water

1 package (4-serving size) JELL-O Brand Cranberry Flavor Sugar Free Low Calorie Gelatin Dessert *or* any red fruit flavor

½ cup cold water

1 can (8 ounces) peach slices in juice, drained, chopped

1 package (4-serving size) JELL-O Brand Orange Flavor Sugar Free Low Calorie Gelatin Dessert

1 can (8 ounces) crushed pineapple in juice, undrained

NUTRITION INFORMATION PER SERVING: 30 calories, 0 g fat, 0 mg cholesterol, 60 mg sodium, 6 g carbohydrate, 0 g dietary fiber, 7 g sugars, 1 g protein

MANDARIN
ORANGE MOLD

Double your pleasure with this two-layer classic. To make picture-perfect angled layers, see the directions on page 8.

see the directions on page 8.

serves **10**

PREP TIME: 20 MIN.
REFRIGERATING TIME: 6 HRS.

Stir boiling water into gelatin in large bowl at least 2 minutes until completely dissolved. Reserve 1 cup gelatin at room temperature. Stir cold water and oranges into remaining gelatin. Pour into 5-cup mold. Refrigerate about 2 hours or until set but not firm (should stick to finger when touched).

Stir yogurt into reserved 1 cup gelatin with wire whisk until smooth. Pour over gelatin layer in mold.

Refrigerate 4 hours or until firm. Unmold. Garnish as desired.

2 cups boiling water

1 package (8-serving size) *or* 2 packages (4-serving size) JELL-O Brand Orange Flavor Sugar Free Low Calorie Gelatin Dessert

¾ cup cold water

1 can (11 ounces) mandarin orange segments, drained

1 container (8 ounces) vanilla lowfat yogurt

NUTRITION INFORMATION PER SERVING: 40 calories, 0 g fat, less than 5 mg cholesterol, 65 mg sodium, 7 g carbohydrate, 0 g dietary fiber, 6 g sugars, 2 g protein, 20% daily value vitamin C

When you're looking for light salad alternatives for holiday menus, this red and green beauty is a jolly solution.

2 cups boiling water

1 package (4-serving size) JELL-O Brand Lime Flavor Sugar Free Low Calorie Gelatin Dessert

½ cup cold water

1 package (4-serving size) JELL-O Brand Strawberry Flavor Sugar Free Low Calorie Gelatin Dessert

1 package (10 ounces) frozen strawberries in lite syrup, partially thawed

1 container (8 ounces) vanilla lowfat yogurt

NUTRITION INFORMATION PER SERVING: 60 calories, 0 g fat, less than 5 mg cholesterol, 65 mg sodium, 11 g carbohydrate, less than 1 g dietary fiber, 9 g sugars, 2 g protein, 15% daily value vitamin C

serves **10**
PREP TIME: 20 MIN.
REFRIGERATING TIME: 4¾ HRS.

Stir 1 cup of the boiling water into lime gelatin in medium bowl at least 2 minutes until completely dissolved. Stir in cold water. Refrigerate about 45 minutes or until slightly thickened (consistency of unbeaten egg whites).

Meanwhile, stir remaining 1 cup boiling water into strawberry gelatin in medium bowl at least 2 minutes until completely dissolved. Add strawberries; stir until thawed. Pour into 5-cup mold. Refrigerate 15 minutes or until set but not firm (should stick to finger when touched).

Stir yogurt into lime gelatin with wire whisk until smooth. Spoon over gelatin layer in mold.

Refrigerate 4 hours or until firm. Unmold. Garnish as desired.

Aloha! A dash of ginger, crushed pineapple and ginger ale turn this simple lime mold into a Polynesian pleasure.

serves 10
PREP TIME: 15 MIN.
REFRIGERATING TIME: 4 HRS.

Stir boiling water into gelatin in large bowl at least 2 minutes until completely dissolved. Stir in pineapple with juice, ginger ale and ginger. Pour into 5-cup mold.

Refrigerate 4 hours or until firm. Unmold. Garnish as desired.

1½ **cups boiling water**

1 **package (8-serving size)** *or*
2 packages (4-serving size) JELL-O Brand Lime Flavor Sugar Free Low Calorie Gelatin Dessert

1 **can (20 ounces) crushed pineapple in juice, undrained**

1 **cup cold diet ginger ale** *or* **club soda**

¼ **teaspoon ground ginger**

NUTRITION INFORMATION PER SERVING: 40 calories, 0 g fat, 0 mg cholesterol, 50 mg sodium, 9 g carbohydrate, 0 g dietary fiber, 8 g sugars, 1 g protein

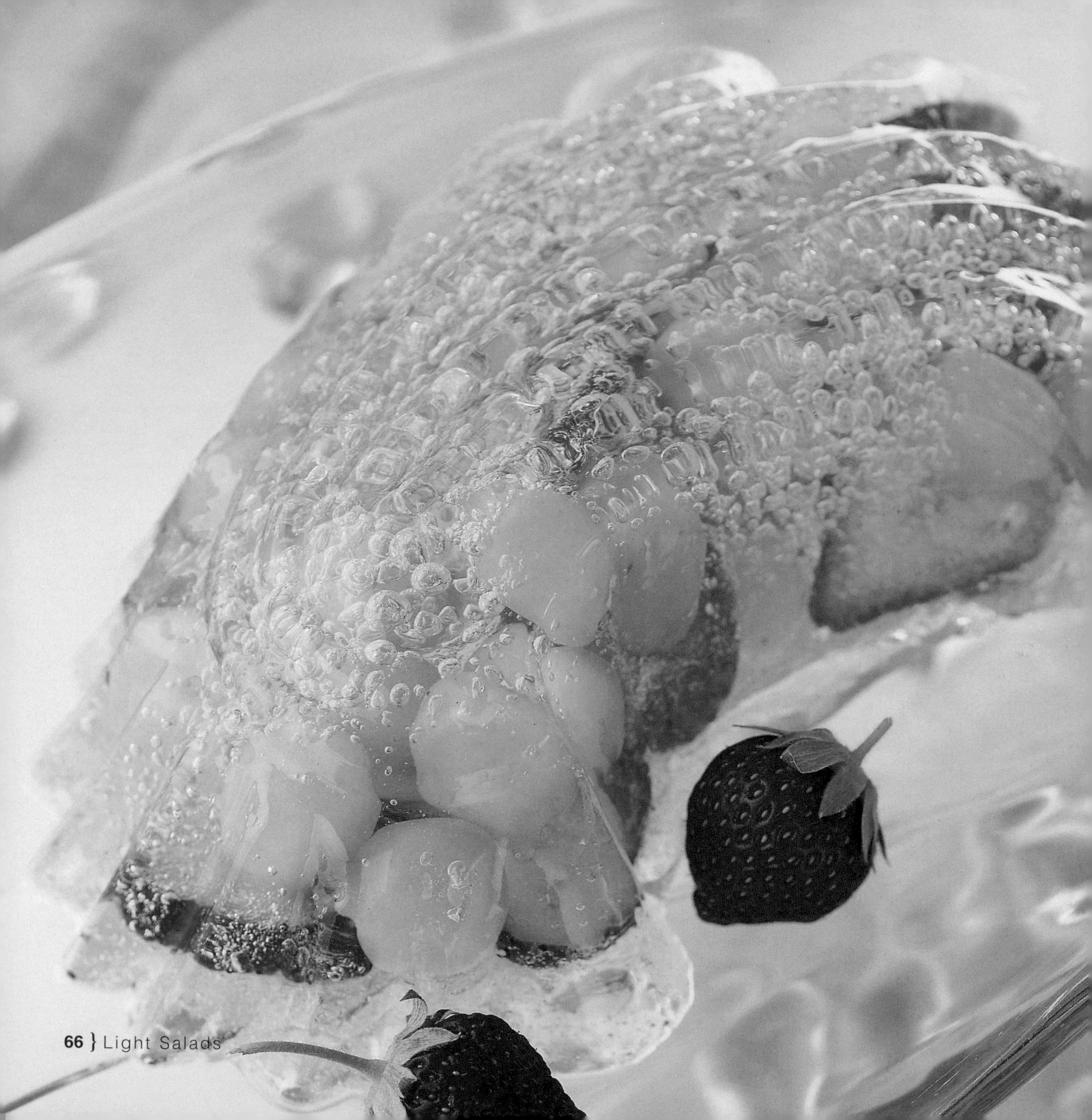

Dry white wine and citrus juices add a special, sophisticated flavor to this sensational mold.

serves 12

PREP TIME: 15 MIN.
REFRIGERATING TIME: 4 HRS.

Bring wine to boil in small saucepan. Stir boiling wine into gelatin in medium bowl at least 2 minutes until completely dissolved. Stir in cold club soda, lime juice and orange juice. Place bowl of gelatin in larger bowl of ice and water. Let stand about 10 minutes or until thickened (spoon drawn through leaves definite impression), stirring occasionally.

Stir in grapes and strawberries. Pour into three 2-cup molds or one 6-cup mold.

Refrigerate 4 hours or until firm. Unmold. Garnish as desired.

1 **cup dry white wine**

1 **package (8-serving size) *or*
2 packages (4-serving size) JELL-O
Brand Lemon Flavor Sugar Free
Low Calorie Gelatin Dessert**

3 **cups cold club soda *or* seltzer**

1 **tablespoon lime juice**

1 **tablespoon orange juice *or*
orange liqueur**

1 **cup green *and/or* red grape halves**

1 **cup sliced strawberries**

NUTRITION INFORMATION PER SERVING: 35 calories,
0 g fat, 0 mg cholesterol, 50 mg sodium,
4 g carbohydrate, less than 1 g dietary fiber,
3 g sugars, 1 g protein, 15% daily value vitamin C

Vegetable Trio Mold
(recipe, page 74)

Lemony Chicken Salad
(recipe, page 71)

SAVORY
SELECTIONS

When it's your turn to bring the appetizer or salad, turn to these refreshing ideas. These tempting JELL-O Gelatin dishes will impress the whole crowd.

For an impressive presentation, garnish this creamy JELL-O mold with thin strips of red pepper.

serves
12

PREP TIME: 15 MIN.
REFRIGERATING TIME: 3 HRS.

Stir boiling water into gelatin in small bowl at least 2 minutes until completely dissolved. Stir in lemon juice, Worcestershire sauce and salt.

Beat cottage cheese, cream cheese and sour cream in large bowl with electric mixer on low speed until smooth. Gradually beat in gelatin mixture. Pour into 4-cup mold.

Refrigerate 3 hours or until firm. Unmold. Garnish as desired. Serve as an appetizer with assorted crackers and raw vegetables.

¾   **cup boiling water**

1   **package (4-serving size) JELL-O Brand Lemon Flavor Gelatin Dessert**

1   **teaspoon lemon juice**

1   **teaspoon Worcestershire sauce**

½   **teaspoon salt**

1   **container (16 ounces) BREAKSTONE'S** *or* **KNUDSEN Cottage Cheese**

1   **tub (8 ounces) PHILADELPHIA FLAVORS Chive & Onion Cream Cheese**

½   **cup BREAKSTONE'S** *or* **KNUDSEN Sour Cream**

VEGETABLE
TRIO MOLD

This flavorful mold is impressive served as a salad or with crackers as a prelude to a fancy dinner *(photo, pages 68-69)*.

2 cups boiling water

1 package (8-serving size) *or*
2 packages (4-serving size) JELL-O
Brand Lemon Flavor Gelatin Dessert

½ teaspoon salt

1½ cups cold water

3 tablespoons vinegar

1¼ cups grated carrots

½ cup KRAFT Mayo Real Mayonnaise
or MIRACLE WHIP Salad Dressing

1 cup shredded zucchini

¼ cup sliced green onions

serves **10** PREP TIME: 30 MIN.
REFRIGERATING TIME: 4¾ HRS.

Stir boiling water into gelatin and salt in large bowl at least 2 minutes until completely dissolved. Stir in cold water and vinegar. Reserve 2¾ cups gelatin at room temperature. Refrigerate remaining gelatin about 1 hour or until thickened (spoon drawn through leaves definite impression).

Stir carrots into thickened gelatin. Spoon into 5-cup mold. Refrigerate about 15 minutes or until set but not firm (should stick to finger when touched).

Stir 1 cup of the reserved gelatin into mayonnaise in medium bowl with wire whisk until smooth. Spoon over gelatin in mold. Refrigerate about 30 minutes or until set but not firm (should stick to finger when touched). Stir zucchini and green onions into remaining reserved gelatin. Spoon over gelatin in mold.

Refrigerate 3 hours or until firm. Unmold. Garnish as desired.

GAZPACHO
SALAD

Like the Mexican chilled soup that was the inspiration for this salad, this marvelous dish turns an ordinary gathering into a fiesta.

serves **6**

PREP TIME: 20 MIN.
REFRIGERATING TIME: 4¼ HRS.

Mix vegetables, vinegar, black pepper and garlic powder in medium bowl; set aside.

Bring tomato juice to boil in small saucepan. Stir into gelatin in large bowl at least 2 minutes until gelatin is completely dissolved. Refrigerate 1¼ hours or until slightly thickened (consistency of unbeaten egg whites).

Stir in vegetable mixture. Pour into 4-cup mold. Refrigerate 3 hours or until firm. Unmold. Serve with salad greens, if desired. Garnish as desired.

1 **cup diced tomato**

½ **cup diced peeled cucumber**

¼ **cup diced green bell pepper**

2 **tablespoons diced red bell pepper**

2 **tablespoons thinly sliced green onions**

2 **tablespoons vinegar**

¼ **teaspoon ground black pepper**

⅛ **teaspoon garlic powder**

1½ **cups tomato juice**

1 **package (4-serving size) JELL-O Brand Lemon Flavor Gelatin Dessert**

THREE
PEPPER
SALAD

Pepper lovers will enjoy the distinctive tart-and-sweet taste combination in this colorful salad. It's terrific with meat, fish or poultry.

serves **10** PREP TIME: 20 MIN.
REFRIGERATING TIME: 5½ HRS.

2 **cups boiling water**

1 **package (8-serving size)** *or*
  **2 packages (4-serving size) JELL-O
  Brand Lemon Flavor Gelatin Dessert**

1½ **cups cold water**

2 **tablespoons lemon juice**

2 **cups chopped red, green** *and/or*
  yellow bell peppers

2 **tablespoons sliced green onions**

Stir boiling water into gelatin in large bowl at least 2 minutes until completely dissolved. Stir in cold water and lemon juice. Refrigerate about 1½ hours or until thickened (spoon drawn through leaves definite impression).

Stir in bell peppers and green onions. Pour into 5-cup mold.

Refrigerate 4 hours or until firm. Unmold. Garnish as desired.

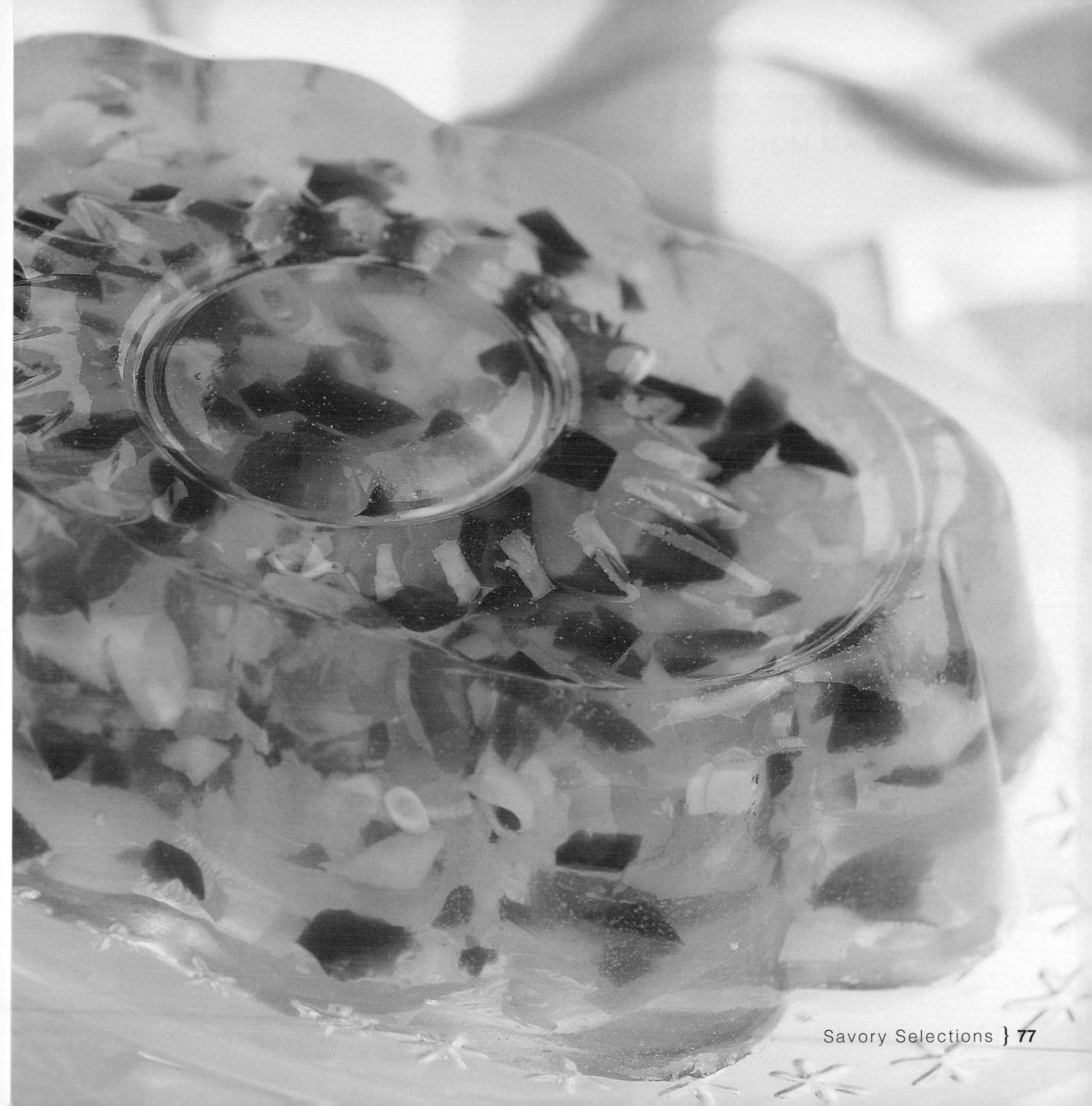

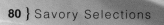

LAYERED
PEAR CHEESE MOLD

When the layers are molded on an angle, this savory-and-sweet mold is as dramatic as it is delicious (*see the directions on page 8*).

serves **10**   PREP TIME: 30 MIN.
REFRIGERATING TIME: 5 HRS.

Drain pears, reserving syrup. Dice pears; set aside. Add water to syrup to measure 1½ cups; bring to boil in small saucepan.

Stir boiling liquid into gelatin in large bowl at least 2 minutes until completely dissolved. Stir in cold ginger ale and lemon juice. Reserve 2½ cups gelatin at room temperature. Pour remaining gelatin into 5-cup mold. Refrigerate about 30 minutes or until thickened (spoon drawn through leaves definite impression). Arrange some of the diced pears in mold.

Meanwhile, stir reserved 2½ cups gelatin gradually into cream cheese in large bowl with wire whisk until smooth. Refrigerate about 30 minutes or until slightly thickened (consistency of unbeaten egg whites). Stir in remaining diced pears and pecans. Spoon over gelatin in mold.

Refrigerate 4 hours or until firm. Unmold.

1   **can (16 ounces) pear halves in syrup, undrained**

    Water

1   **package (8-serving size)** *or* **2 packages (4-serving size) JELL-O Brand Lime Flavor Gelatin Dessert**

½   **cup cold ginger ale** *or* water

2   **tablespoons lemon juice**

1   **package (8 ounces) PHILADELPHIA Cream Cheese, softened**

¼   **cup chopped pecans**

Crown Jewel Dessert *(recipe, page 85)* and
Ambrosia Tropical Mold *(recipe, page 84)*

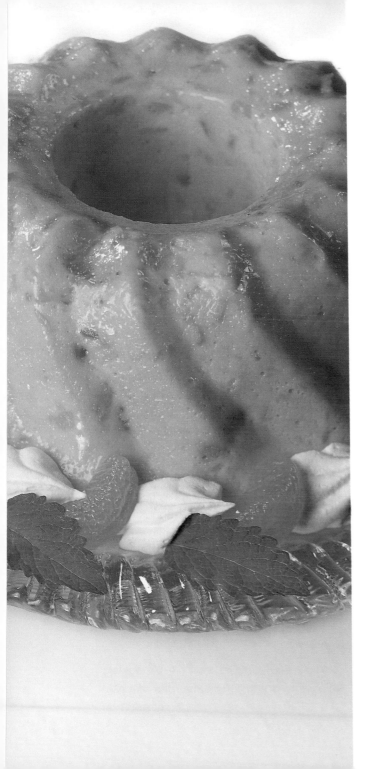

CLASSIC
MOLDS

Remember your mother's delicious gelatin creations? You can make molds like hers with these traditional delights, revised for the way you cook today.

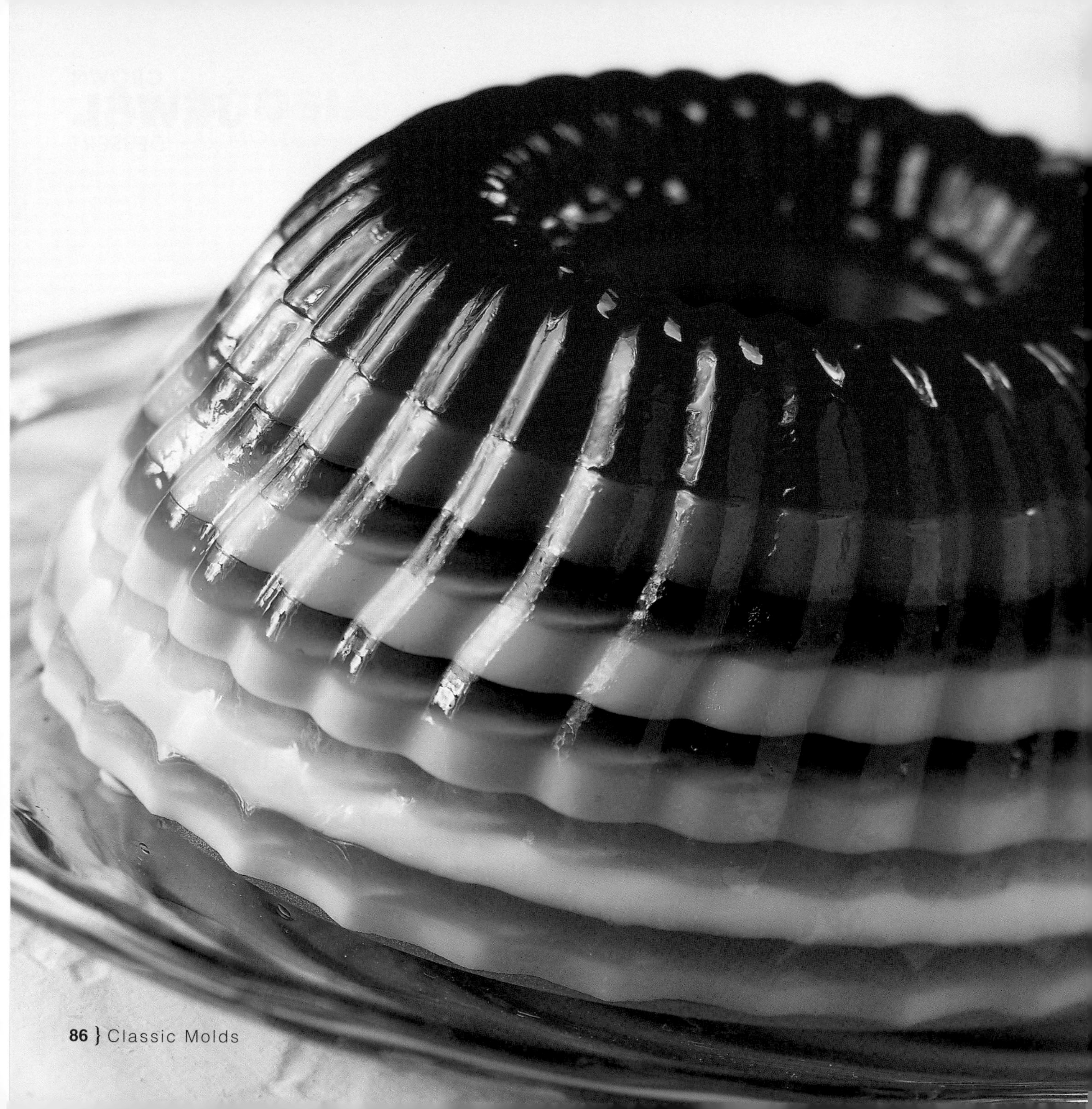

RAINBOW
RIBBON MOLD

Wow your family and friends with this gorgeous
10-layer JELL-O mold.

serves
12

PREP TIME: 1 HR.
REFRIGERATING TIME: 5 HRS.

Stir 1¼ cups boiling water into 1 flavor of gelatin in small bowl at least 2 minutes until completely dissolved. Pour ¾ cup dissolved gelatin into 6-cup mold. Refrigerate about 15 minutes or until set but not firm (should stick to finger when touched). Refrigerate remaining gelatin in bowl about 5 minutes or until slightly thickened (consistency of unbeaten egg whites). Gradually stir in 3 tablespoons of the sour cream. Spoon over gelatin layer in mold. Refrigerate about 15 minutes or until set but not firm (should stick to finger when touched).

Repeat process with each remaining gelatin flavor. (Be sure to cool dissolved gelatin to room temperature before pouring into mold.) Refrigerate gelatin as directed to create a total of 10 alternating clear and creamy gelatin layers.

Refrigerate 2 hours or until firm. Unmold.

6¼ **cups boiling water**

5 **packages (4-serving size) JELL-O Brand Gelatin Dessert, any 5 different fruit flavors**

1 **cup (½ pint) BREAKSTONE'S Sour Cream *or* vanilla lowfat yogurt**

Packed with nutrients from carrots and pineapple, this creamy, orange mold tastes fantastic with nutty whole-grain muffins.

serves **10** PREP TIME: 20 MIN.
REFRIGERATING TIME: 6 HRS.

2   **cups boiling water**

1   **package (8-serving size) or
2 packages (4-serving size) JELL-O
Brand Orange Flavor Gelatin Dessert**

¼   **cup cold water**

1   **can (8 ounces) crushed pineapple
in juice, undrained**

1   **cup shredded carrots**

1   **container (8 ounces) vanilla lowfat
yogurt**

Stir boiling water into gelatin in large bowl at least 2 minutes until completely dissolved. Reserve 1 cup of the gelatin at room temperature. Stir cold water, pineapple with juice and carrots into remaining gelatin. Spoon into 5-cup mold. Refrigerate about 2 hours or until set but not firm (should stick to finger when touched).

Stir yogurt into reserved 1 cup gelatin with wire whisk until smooth. Pour over gelatin layer in mold.

Refrigerate 4 hours or until firm. Unmold. Garnish as desired.

RIBBON
SQUARES

This all-time favorite features three ribbons of JELL-O Gelatin, cream cheese and fruit. Cut it into squares to show off the layers.

3   **cups boiling water**

1   **package (4-serving size) JELL-O Brand Gelatin Dessert, any red fruit flavor**

1   **package (4-serving size) JELL-O Brand Lemon Flavor Gelatin Dessert**

1   **package (4-serving size) JELL-O Brand Lime Flavor Gelatin Dessert**

1½   **cups cold water**

1   **package (8 ounces) PHILADELPHIA Cream Cheese, softened**

1   **can (8 ounces) crushed pineapple in juice, undrained**

1   **cup thawed COOL WHIP Whipped Topping**

½   **cup KRAFT Mayo Real Mayonnaise**

serves
9

PREP TIME: 30 MIN.
REFRIGERATING TIME: 5¼ HRS.

Stir 1 cup of the boiling water into each flavor of gelatin in separate medium bowls at least 2 minutes until completely dissolved. Stir ¾ cup of the cold water into red gelatin. Pour into 9-inch square pan. Refrigerate about 45 minutes or until set but not firm (should stick to finger when touched).

Meanwhile, stir lemon gelatin mixture gradually into cream cheese until smooth. Stir in pineapple with juice. Refrigerate about 45 minutes or until slightly thickened (consistency of unbeaten egg whites). Stir in whipped topping and mayonnaise. Spoon over red gelatin layer in pan. Refrigerate about 30 minutes or until set but not firm.

Meanwhile, stir remaining ¾ cup cold water into lime gelatin. Refrigerate about 30 minutes or until slightly thickened. Spoon over lemon gelatin mixture in pan.

Refrigerate 4 hours or until firm. Unmold.

JELL-O Gelatin Lemon Flavor adds new dimension to this favorite. Garnish with sliced apples dipped in lemon juice.

serves **10**

PREP TIME: 20 MIN.
REFRIGERATING TIME: 5½ HRS.

Stir boiling water into gelatin in large bowl at least 2 minutes until completely dissolved. Stir in cold water and lemon juice. Refrigerate about 1½ hours or until thickened (spoon drawn through leaves definite impression).

Gradually stir in mayonnaise with wire whisk. Stir in apple, celery and walnuts. Pour into 5-cup mold.

Refrigerate 4 hours or until firm. Unmold. Serve on salad greens, if desired. Garnish as desired.

2   cups boiling water

1   package (8-serving size) *or*
     2 packages (4-serving size) JELL-O
     Brand Lemon Flavor Gelatin Dessert

1   cup cold water

1   tablespoon lemon juice

½   cup KRAFT Mayo Real Mayonnaise
     or MIRACLE WHIP Salad Dressing

1   medium red apple, diced

½   cup diced celery

¼   cup chopped walnuts

INDEX

INDEX

METRIC
CONVERSIONS

Metric Cooking Hints

By making a few conversions, cooks in Australia, Canada and the United Kingdom can use these recipes with confidence. The charts on this page provide a guide for converting measurements from the U.S. customary system, which is used throughout this book, to the imperial and metric systems. There also is a conversion table for oven temperatures to accommodate the differences in oven calibrations.

Product Differences: Most of the ingredients called for in recipes are available in English-speaking countries. However, some are known by different names. Here are some common American ingredients and their possible counterparts:

- Sugar is granulated or castor sugar.
- Powdered sugar is icing sugar.
- All-purpose flour is plain household flour or white flour. When self-rising flour is used in place of all-purpose flour in a recipe that calls for leavening, omit the leavening agent (baking soda or baking powder) and salt.
- Light-colored corn syrup is golden syrup.
- Cornstarch is cornflour.
- Baking soda is bicarbonate of soda.
- Vanilla is vanilla essence.
- Green, red or yellow bell peppers are capsicums.
- Golden raisins are sultanas.

Volume and Weight: Americans traditionally use cup measures for liquid and solid ingredients. The chart, at right, shows the approximate imperial and metric equivalents. If you are accustomed to weighing solid ingredients, the following approximate equivalents will be helpful.

- 1 cup butter, castor sugar or rice = 8 ounces = about 250 grams
- 1 cup flour = 4 ounces = about 125 grams
- 1 cup icing sugar = 5 ounces = about 150 grams

Spoon measures are used for smaller amounts of ingredients. Although the size of the tablespoon varies slightly in different countries, for practical purposes and for recipes in this book, a straight substitution is all that's necessary.

Measurements made using cups or spoons should always be level unless stated otherwise.

Equivalents: U.S.=Australia/U.K.

⅛ teaspoon = 0.5 ml	⅔ cup = ½ cup = 5 fluid ounces = 150 ml
¼ teaspoon = 1 ml	¾ cup = ⅔ cup = 6 fluid ounces = 180 ml
½ teaspoon = 2 ml	1 cup = ¾ cup = 8 fluid ounces = 240 ml
1 teaspoon = 5 ml	1¼ cups = 1 cup
1 tablespoon = 1 tablespoon	2 cups = 1 pint
¼ cup = 2 tablespoons = 2 fluid ounces = 60 ml	1 quart = 1 l
⅓ cup = ¼ cup = 3 fluid ounces = 90 ml	½ inch =1.27 cm
½ cup = ⅓ cup = 4 fluid ounces = 120 ml	1 inch = 2.54 cm

Baking Pan Sizes

American	Metric
8x1½-inch round baking pan	20x4-cm cake tin
9x1½-inch round baking pan	23x3.5-cm cake tin
11x7x1½-inch baking pan	28x18x4-cm baking tin
13x9x2-inch baking pan	30x20x3-cm baking tin
2-quart rectangular baking dish	30x20x3-cm baking tin
15x10x1-inch baking pan	30x25x2-cm baking tin (Swiss roll tin)
9-inch pie plate	22x4- or 23x4-cm pie plate
7- or 8-inch springform pan	18- or 20-cm springform or loose-bottom cake tin
9x5x3-inch loaf pan	23x13x7-cm or 2-pound narrow loaf tin or pâté tin
1½-quart casserole	1.5-l casserole
2-quart casserole	2-l casserole

Oven Temperature Equivalents

Fahrenheit Setting	Celsius Setting*	Gas Setting
300°F	150°C	Gas Mark 2 (slow)
325°F	160°C	Gas Mark 3 (moderately slow)
350°F	180°C	Gas Mark 4 (moderate)
375°F	190°C	Gas Mark 5 (moderately hot)
400°F	200°C	Gas Mark 6 (hot)
425°F	220°C	Gas Mark 7
450°F	230°C	Gas Mark 8 (very hot)
Broil		Grill

* Electric and gas ovens may be calibrated using Celsius. However, for an electric oven, increase the Celsius setting 10 to 20 degrees when cooking above 160°C. For convection or forced-air ovens (gas or electric), lower the temperature setting 10°C when cooking at all heat levels.